Working with Others

Katie Peters

GRL Consultants,
Diane Craig and Monica Marx,
Certified Literacy Specialists

Lerner Publications ◆ Minneapolis

Note from a GRL Consultant
This Pull Ahead leveled book has been carefully designed for beginning readers.
A team of guided reading literacy experts has reviewed and leveled the book to
ensure readers pull ahead and experience success.

Lerner Publications Company
An imprint of Lerner Publishing Group, Inc.
241 First Avenue North
Minneapolis, MN 55401 USA

For reading levels and more information, look up this title at www.lernerbooks.com.

Main body text set in Memphis Pro 24/39
Typeface provided by Linotype.

Photo Acknowledgments
The images in this book are used with the permission of: © 3sbworld/Getty Images, p. 3;
© FatCamera/Getty Images, pp. 4–5, 16 (soccer ball); © fizkes/Getty Images, pp. 12–13;
© fstop123/Getty Images, pp. 6–7, 16 (flower); © karens4/Getty Images, pp. 10–11;
© MichaelSvoboda/Getty Images, pp. 14–15, 16 (pail); © SDI Productions/Getty Images, pp. 8–9.

Front cover: © hadynyah/Getty Images

Library of Congress Cataloging-in-Publication Data

Names: Peters, Katie, author.
Title: Working with others / Katie Peters.
Description: Minneapolis : Lerner Publications, 2022. | Series: Helpful habits. Pull ahead readers.
   People smarts. Non fiction. | Includes index. | Audience: Ages 4–7 | Audience: Grades K–1 |
   Summary: "Support young readers as they learn the key skill of working with others every day on
   a variety of projects. Pairs with the fiction title Lola and Lupe's House"— Provided by publisher.
Identifiers: LCCN 2020015310 (print) | LCCN 2020015311 (ebook) | ISBN 9781728403496
   (library binding) | ISBN 9781728423234 (paperback) | ISBN 9781728418391 (ebook)
Subjects: LCSH: Cooperativeness in children—Juvenile literature. | Cooperativeness—
   Juvenile literature.
Classification: LCC BF723.C69 P47 2021 (print) | LCC BF723.C69 (ebook) | DDC 155.4/192—dc23

LC record available at https://lccn.loc.gov/2020015310
LC ebook record available at https://lccn.loc.gov/2020015311

Manufactured in the United States of America
1 - 48345 - 48887 - 1/22/2021

Table of Contents

Working with Others

We play soccer together.

We plant flowers together.

We make a robot together.

We do a puzzle together.

We bake cookies together.

We build a castle together.

Can you think of a time when you worked with others?

Did You See It?

flower

pail

soccer ball

Index